LAMPSHADES
Simple and Advanced

BY

MARGARET ROURKE

MILLS & BOON LIMITED, LONDON

Published in this edition by Mills & Boon Limited,
17-19 Foley Street, London W1A 1DR

© LAMPSHADES Margaret Rourke 1960
Reprinted 1963
Reprinted 1965
Reprinted (new edition) 1967

© ADVANCED LAMPSHADES Margaret Rourke 1961

This combined edition 1969
Reprinted 1972

ISBN 0 263.51376.9

Printed in Great Britain by Butler & Tanner Ltd.,
Frome and London

CONTENTS

INTRODUCTION

THIS book will help you to produce some attractive lampshades, which, if they were bought, would be very expensive. A selection has been made to give a variation in styles, suitable for most of your rooms; it includes some new ideas from the Continent, and these have been adapted and worked out in materials which are easily obtainable in this country. Although a few of these shades may, at first sight, appear to be a little complicated, you should have no difficulty in achieving a satisfactory result, if you follow the instructions carefully.

There are many different shapes in frames, and each new one is shown with the diagram for the lampshade for which it is used as a foundation. It cannot be emphasized too often that the frame is the most important part of your work, and it is as well to choose a frame made of a good firm wire, especially when you are making a large or standard size. The bowed Empire shape is a good classical design; it is suitable for all sizes, lends itself well to most types of decoration and is one of the easiest shapes to cover. But do try some of the more unusual shapes, which you will find illustrated.

Before starting the covering, it is necessary to bind your wire frame, and always make sure that the binding is as tight as you can make it; you will find it easier, when binding the larger frames, to divide the tape needed for the base into two halves, so as to avoid having to work with a long length of tape. Different materials, new techniques, exciting ideas in trimmings, bedlights, shades with removable coverings for easy laundering, the use of velvet and brocade, embroidery, these and many other up-to-date ideas for lampshades will add a great deal of pleasure to your craftwork. With your usual sewing needs at hand, some imagination plus a little care and patience will produce lampshades of surprising excellence.

TOOLS AND EQUIPMENT

The tools and equipment needed are simple and most can already be found in your work basket:

Strong Needles and smaller needles called "betweens" for fabric shades.

Spring Clothes Pegs for use with plastic shades.

Scissors for cutting-out and a smaller pair for trimming seams and turnings.

Sewing Thread to match the material.

Steel Pins in plentiful supply.

Tape for binding the frame. This is a poor quality tape which can be bought specially for this purpose in white, natural and pink. If you prefer to match the colour of your shade you can use Prussian binding which can be obtained in a number of colours. To get a really first class finish, however, you can use Jap silk cut into strips.

Lampshade Frames. These are so inexpensive that I seldom think it worth while to use an old one for re-covering, as the latter will often be found to be slightly rusty when the wires are unbound.

Material to cover the frame. In this book we shall be dealing with plastics, fabrics, laces and buckram, all of which are very suitable for making lampshades.

Before you begin to work you will need to decide for what purpose you intend to use your shade. You can only choose your frame when you have decided whether it is just for decoration, for a reading light or to lighten a dark corner in the room; whether it is to be a bright contemporary shade or an elegant lace or georgette one to match in with some antique furniture.

CHOOSING A FRAME

THE frame and its fittings are your first consideration because they are the foundation of the lampshade, and so, to begin with, you need a good firm wire frame in the shape and size of your choice. There are very many classical and modern styles and you will find a varied and attractive selection at most craft shops. If you cannot find exactly what you need it is possible to have a frame made to your own special design at a good handicraft shop. Some of the more popular shapes are shown on the opposite page and these are the types of frames we shall cover in different materials, in easy and attractive ways.

Square Frame (diag. 1) with straight side wires (these are sometimes called staves) and square at the top and base.

Coolie type Frame (diag. 2) has a narrow collar round the top of the frame.

Straight Empire Frame (diag. 3) with straight sides and the top and base rings either round or oval.

Bowed Empire Frame (diag. 4) similar to No. 3 but with the side wires or staves curved inwards.

Drum Frame (diag. 5) with the top and base rings the same size and obtainable with either straight or bowed side wires.

The fitting attaches the frame either to the bulb or to its holder. The pendant is for a hanging light and the adjustable gimbal for a table lamp, allowing the shade to be adjusted to any angle as required; this fitting can also be used for a pendant light. The butterfly fitting, two circular wires which fit on to the lamp, is for small shades and can also be adjusted if necessary. The duplex ring is used for large table lamps and standard shades; this is placed on a gimbal fitting attached to the lampstand.

Frames are sold in many sizes from a few inches upwards and are measured across the base ring as in diag. 3. Always make sure that your frame is of the correct size and shape for its purpose, and if you are making a shade for a table lamp it is advisable to take the stand with you when you buy the frame.

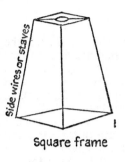

Square frame

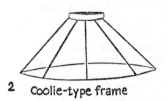

2 Coolie-type frame

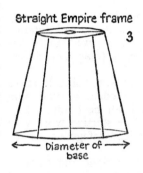

Straight Empire frame
3

Bowed Empire frame
4

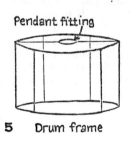

5 Drum frame

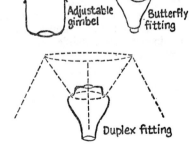

7

BINDING

HAVING chosen your frame, the next step is the binding. The materials you need for a 10″ or 12″ frame are 6 to 8 yards of lampshade binding tape or Prussian binding. Bind the side wires first, but leave one unbound (diag. 1), and then bind round the top ring and down the unbound wire, finishing at the base (diag. 2). You then complete the binding by covering the base ring. For each side wire you will need a piece of tape one and a half times the length of the wire, and for the top and base rings about twice the length. Cut off the tape as you need it. When cutting off the tape for the top, do not forget to allow twice round the top ring AND one and a half times for the unbound side wire.

Start by turning over the tape about 1″ over the top ring and finish with a knot at the base (diags. 3 and 4). Binding the top and base rings is done in the same way, but cover the joins of the wires with a figure of eight (diag. 5) and then finish with the knot just described.

Jap silk binding is done in the same way, using 1″ strips doubled lengthways, covering the raw edges as you bind (diag. 6). The gimbal fittings should not be bound. You can, if you wish, paint the frame before starting work with a white or cream enamel; it is an added safeguard against rust when the shade is washed.

The binding when finished should be tight and smooth. To test this, take a bound wire between your finger and thumb and try to twist it in both directions. If it moves, it is worth doing the binding again, as this is often the cause of a fabric lampshade slackening; also a badly bound frame (when it is visible, as in a modern plastic shade) can spoil the whole effect. When you are quite satisfied that you have made the best possible job, then you can go ahead with the covering.

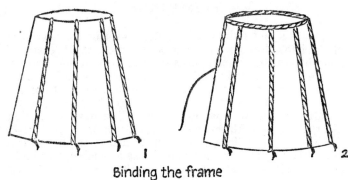

Binding the frame

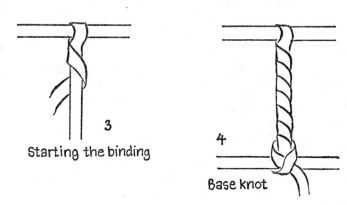

3

Starting the binding

4

Base knot

5

Covering the joins

6

Using Jap Silk

TRIMMINGS

COVERINGS and linings will be dealt with in the later part of the book, but since trimmings—the most exciting part of lampshade making—can be used on all these shades as they are made, it will be helpful to have a word about them first.

The covering can be quite simple but the right trimming can make your lampshade look really expensive. There are countless attractive ways to do this. You have a selection of braids, gimps, fringes, tassel fringes, bobble fringes, velvet ribbons, nylon frillings, ric-rac, cords and laces, or you can use a piece of the covering material as a binding (this looks good on tailored plain shades) or try the effect of combining two different trimmings. Here is the way to sew them on:

Braids, Gimps etc. should be sewn as diag. 1, using a long stitch which attaches the braid to the frame, just catching in the top and bottom edges of the braid. These are useful to cover the side wires on plastic shades and also round the top and base of fabric shades.

Material, Velvet Ribbons etc. should be oversewn along the edge of the frame. These sometimes look well if they are caught down at intervals as diags. 2 and 4.

Fringes and Bobble Fringes sometimes have a braid attached. If they have not you must fix a braid to cover the heading.

An interesting finish for contemporary shades is to trim them with thick piping cord—this is very inexpensive—attached to form loops along the edge (diag. 5). Appliquéd motifs are very effective, especially for nursery shades, making use of nursery rhyme characters, engines etc., cut from materials (diag. 6); or an individual touch could be an embroidered panel on a fabric shade.

There are many fabric adhesives on the market today which are useful for attaching decorations to lampshades where stitching would be unsightly, and adhesive is most helpful if a small spot is put on the ends of a braid or fringe which is inclined to fray.

Always measure accurately round the frame for the amount of trimming you need. Do this with a tape measure, and allow an *extra* inch rather than underestimate. Should you find you are an inch or so short of braid or fringe, hold the length in the steam of a kettle for a few minutes and then give it a good firm stretch; you will usually find that this treatment will give you that extra inch that you need.

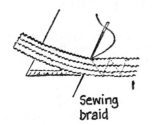

Sewing braid

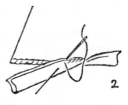

Attaching material

Attaching braid to bobble fringe

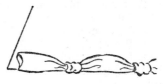

Velvet ribbon

Piping cord trimming

Appliquéd motifs

MATERIALS AND FINISHES

THE following are suggestions for covering the frames mentioned in this book—damask, brocade, fine linen, velvet, glazed chintz and also those materials which have metallic threads in their weave. Raffia is another material which has become very popular for modern shades. Many traditional weaves are now reproduced in synthetic materials.

Some of the lampshades which you will be making will need to have a trimming over the raw edges down the staves, and as a decorative finish, in some cases, would be unsuitable, it is as well to have a note here on how to deal with this problem.

To make a plain neat finish:

1. Cut a bias strip of material one inch wide.
2. Fold into three lengthways (diag. 1).
3. Pin at the top of the stave (diag. 2).
4. Sew just into the surface material by catching in the smallest amount possible, at each side and into the binding (diag. 3).

Sometimes you will find, when you have fitted a balloon lining, that the gimbal fitting has caused the lining to be a little roughly finished. To avoid this, carry out the following work, before the trimming is put on.

1. Take a straight strip of lining material, about one inch wide.
2. Fold in three lengthways and press flat (diag. 4).
3. Place under the gimbal fitting (diag. 5) and then over the top ring, and on to the outside of the cover.
4. Stitch the ends onto the outside of the frame (diag. 6).
5. Cut closely, and then trim the top in the usual way.

You will find that a little time spent on these finishes will be well worth while.

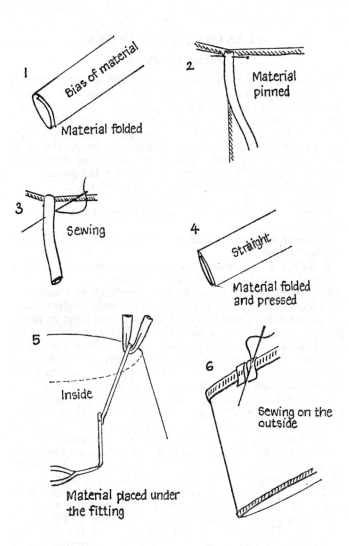

1 Bias of material

Material folded

2 Material pinned

3 Sewing

4 Straight

Material folded and pressed

5 Inside

Material placed under the fitting

6 Sewing on the outside

PLASTIC LAMPSHADES

Making the Pattern

PLASTIC shades are very easy to make and are most suitable for many types of contemporary fittings, and you cannot do better for quick and colourful results. You can obtain plastics in wonderful designs and colours; most of them can be washed or sponged, but do make quite sure of this when you buy your plastic material. They may be purchased by the piece or by the yard. Here is a short list of some of the plastics and boards which are suitable for lampshades.

Laminated linen, cotton or dupion—easy to work.

Matt acetate—a most attractive finish.

Linen-backed acetate—these include very good floral and Jacobean designs etc.

Corduroy embossed polythene—a firm material, looks well on the " Drum ".

Rigid P.V.C.—in many colours and contemporary designs.

Boards printed in colour with stars etc.

Perforated boards—these look particularly well when the light shines through the perforations, in lovely bright colours.

For the pattern you will need an uncreased sheet of brown paper. From this cut a piece slightly larger than one of the panels of the frame. Press over the wires of a panel until you have an impression of the shape (diag. 1). Remove the paper carefully, when you should have a good pattern of the shape. Replace on to the panel to check for accuracy and re-trim until it fits on to the wires without any surplus edges (diag. 2). Try fitting this paper pattern on to each of the other panels, as sometimes there is a variation in size. Should this occur, just make another pattern for the odd panel—but do not forget to mark which one it is! Although a square frame is illustrated, this method of pattern making is suitable for any of the shapes shown on page 7, with one exception, and that is the " Drum ". This would only need the depth to be measured and also the length round the frame, and the material should be cut to this measurement allowing 1″ for joining (diag. 3). Check that top and base rings are the same size.

Accuracy in measuring and cutting your pattern cannot be emphasized too much, and you will find that the time spent on this preliminary work will be well repaid.

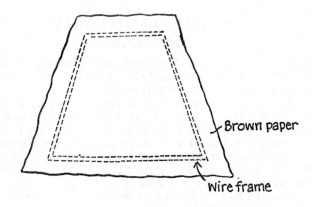

Brown paper

Wire frame

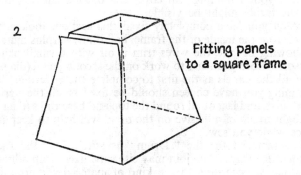

2

Fitting panels
to a square frame

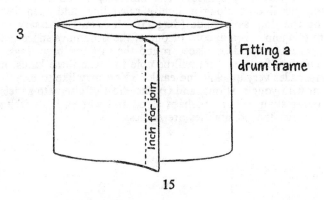

3

Fitting a
drum frame

Inch for join

PLASTIC LAMPSHADES
Making the Shade

PLACE the pattern you have made on the wrong side of the plastic material or board and mark round it with a very soft pencil or crayon. Repeat this until you have the number of sections you need for your shade and then cut them out on the pencil line. It is a good idea to plan this first, as a little rearranging may prove to be an economy of material. Place one section on a panel of the frame and hold it in place with a few spring pegs or clamps (diag. 1) and then sew it on to the bound wires using matching thread (diag. 2). Larger stitches should be used on the outside of the cover and small neat stitches just into the binding on the inside of the frame. Although your trimming will cover the outside stitches, those on the inside might be visible.

When you have completely fixed this section, look at the panel from the inside of the frame, and if any surplus material is showing beyond the wires trim it off with a small pair of scissors before you start to work on the second panel (diag. 3). Sew all the panels as the first to complete the covering. The trimming you have chosen should be fixed to all the upright wires first, and last of all round the top and base rings (diag. 4). A slight touch of adhesive on the braid will help to keep it in place while you sew.

The material for the " Drum " is stitched to the frame in the same way. The join may either be fixed with adhesive or stitched, according to the kind of material you are using. When you are stitching, work with matching thread and keep the stitches evenly spaced. The best way to do this is to place pencil dots along a lightly ruled line, and then sew using the dots as a guide (diag. 5). It is not necessary to trim this join. Braid, cord or one of the trimmings suggested on page 11 should be placed round the top and base rings.

You will find that you will be able to make these kinds of lampshades very quickly and easily. You may like to experiment with your next one, and try the effect of alternate panels in contrasting colours, perhaps a red and white with a white trimming—the possibilities are endless.

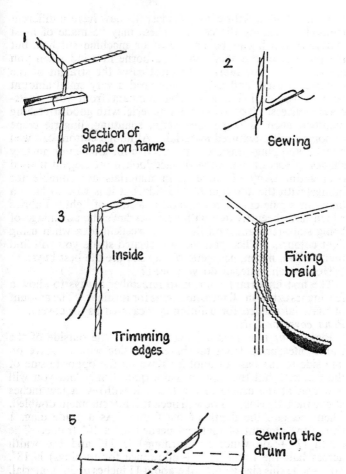

1

Section of
shade on frame

2

Sewing

3

Inside

Trimming
edges

Fixing
braid

5

Sewing the
drum

FABRICS AND HOW TO MEASURE THEM

PROGRESSING to fabric lampshades, we now have a different method of making the cover. These may be made of most materials which can be handsewn or machine stitched, but the purpose of the shade must be borne in mind when you are choosing your fabric. In most cases the straight of the material is used, and as you only need a very small amount perhaps you will find a suitable remnant from your dressmaking pieces. Try to choose a material with good stretching qualities, such as crepe-back satin, shantung, lingerie crepe or some similar textured material. Although cottons can well be used and ginghams are very effective for kitchen or nursery shades, pieces of net, voile or lace look most elegant if used over satin. Any of these plain materials are suitable for linings, with the addition of Jap silk, but it is wise to have a lining in a pale colour for a good reflection of light. Fabrics which have been treated with silicones have the advantage of being stain-resistant, and this is an excellent idea when using light colours. When you make a pleated shade you will find that chiffon, ninon, georgette or Jap silk are the best buys.

How much material do you need?

The first important point is to remember always to allow a few inches extra on all measurements for turnings. The amount of material needed for a lining is measured as for covers.

Plain cover or lining

Place your tape measure across half of the outside of the frame, measuring from the base of a side wire or stave on one side to the base of another stave on the opposite side of the frame. Pull the tape measure quite firmly and you will find that at the centre of the frame it will rest a few inches above the base ring. You will need this measurement doubled. Then measure the depth of the frame. As a guide diag. 1 shows the amount of material needed for a 10″ frame. The depth (7″ + allowance for turnings) is 11″ and the width across half the frame (14″ + allowance for turnings) is 18″. So a shade this size would take about 11 inches of 36″ material.

Pleating (diag. 2)

The amount of material needed will be equal to the depth of the frame and three times round the largest ring. For this 10″ frame, you would require 1 yard of 36″ material for pleating and $\frac{1}{3}$ yard of 36″ for lining.

Swathed pleating

This is measured in the same way as straight pleating, but you must allow sufficient material to pull across a quarter of the frame (diag. 3).

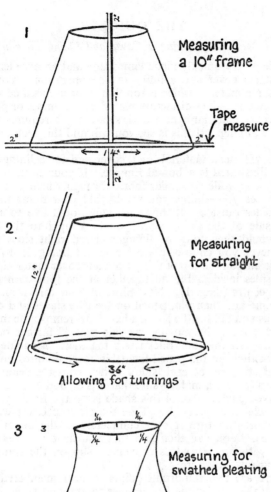

1

Measuring
a 10" frame

Tape
measure

2

Measuring
for straight

Allowing for turnings

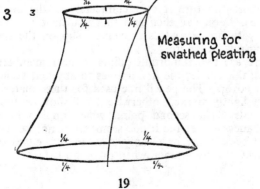

3

Measuring for
swathed pleating

THE QUICKIE

A Method of Fixing a Cover and Lining Together

THIS is a very quickly made lampshade and an excellent way of fixing a cover and a lining in one operation. You may have some material which is too flimsy for use as a cover and yet would be quite satisfactory placed over a lining, or perhaps your cover material is of a dark shade which requires a light coloured lining. If this is so, you will find this method most useful.

You will need material for a cover and for a lining. The shade illustrated is a bowed Empire. If your cover material is of net or voile or similar fabric through which you would like to see your lining, you would fold your lining material right sides outside. If, however, you would like to see the right side of the lining when you look up into the shade, you would then fold the lining material right sides inside. Whichever you choose, place the folded lining on to a flat surface and on the top of this place your cover material folded right sides inside. Pin all together at the four corners and at the centre (diag. 1). Now place all four thicknesses over the frame and then pin, pencil on the side staves and cut the edges as you did for the last shade. Now remove the material from the frame by moving the side pins $\frac{1}{2}''$ farther out and repinning all the four thicknesses together. Machine stitch or backstitch on the pencil line (this cover requires only one row of stitching at each side). Then trim the seam to $\frac{1}{4}''$ turnings (diag. 2), making sure that it is a good clean cut with no frayed edges, as once this shade is on the frame you will be unable to correct this. Take the piece of cover which is uppermost and turn it over completely to the under lining (diag. 3). You will then find that you have a cover and a lining with no raw edges showing. Slip on the frame and pin and sew as before.

There are two important points to be remembered when making this shade; the first applies to any net, voile, lace or similar cover. The pencil line used for these materials must be very lightly marked, otherwise it will show on the finished lampshade. The second point, which applies to all lined lampshades, is that the inside seams must not be wider than $\frac{1}{4}''$ and these must be cleanly cut. Frayed edges can spoil the effect of a lampshade when the lamp is on.

1

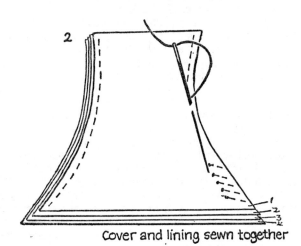

Cover
Lining

Pinning four thicknesses together

2

Cover and lining sewn together

3

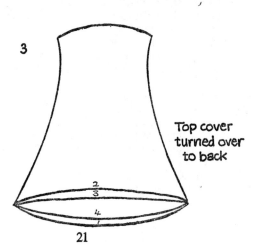

Top cover
turned over
to back

21

AN INEXPENSIVE FABRIC SHADE
WITH A FRENCH SEAM

THE lampshade illustrated (diag. 1) has a glazed cotton cover in yellow and white and is trimmed with white ric-rac braid. The frame is a straight Empire shape. Both the cover material and the trimming are very inexpensive, but any of the materials listed on page 18 could be used.

Having bound the frame, fold your material in half with the right sides outside and then place it against the half of the frame, pinning at the top and base of each side wire, firmly catching in the binding but not pinning round the wire. The straight of the material should be in the centre. Then place a few more pins on the side wires (diag. 2).

Pull material against frame, removing one pin at a time to do this, then replacing pin, until material is tightly stretched across frame. (Staves should have material stretched over them sufficiently to show.) Place pins at the base and put more pins in between the pins at each side until they are about 1″ apart, then cut material away to about 1½″ and slash at sides (diag. 3). Pin around the top.

When material is firmly stretched, take a pencil and mark down on the wire at each side. Remove cover from frame by taking out the side pins and replacing about ½″ farther to the edge. Take out top and base pins (diag. 4). Backstitch or machine stitch first row ⅛″ *outside* pencil line, then cut material closely, turn to the wrong side and French seam on the line. Turn cover to right side. Slip cover over frame and pin seams to frame at top and base, fitting the two seams to two staves. Pin all round base and then pin top.

Stitch cover to frame with oversewing; stitches should just catch the binding and not go round the wire (diag. 5). Turn back raw edges at base, and stitch deeply, working over stitches already there (diag. 6). Slash turnings down to stitches at the top, and stitch in the same way as at the base. Cut all turnings very closely. Sew on your own choice of trimming round the top and base; the side seams do not require any.

This simple method of covering is also suitable for the bowed Empire or square frames.

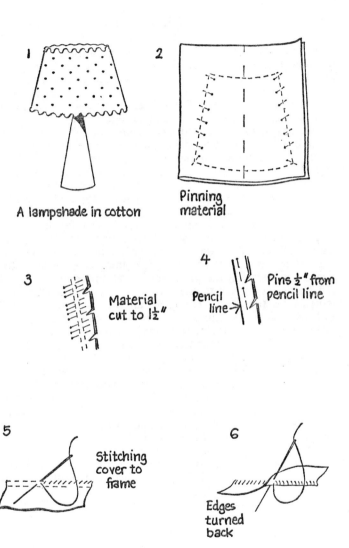

1 A lampshade in cotton

2 Pinning material

3 Material cut to 1½"

4 Pencil line → Pins ½" from pencil line

5 Stitching cover to frame

6 Edges turned back

A PLEATED DRUM

AFTER you have made the plain covered lampshades, now is the time to try some with pleats. This first one is an easy one with which to start as there is no need to line it if you use a fairly firm material such as a crepe-back satin or tussore. If you wish to use one of the listed materials which are of a thinner texture it would of course need a lining.

The lampshade illustrated has a frame 14″ diameter and a depth of 8″ to 9″; for this you would need 1 yard of crepe-back satin. Divide your material into three lengths, $10\frac{1}{2}″ \times 36″$, and three strips, $1\frac{1}{2}″ \times 36″$. These strips will be used for the trimming. Take a piece of the satin and pin a turning the width of a pleat (in this case $\frac{3}{8}″$) at the top and base of a stave (diag. 2). You can make your pleats whatever size you wish, but having made this first one all the following pleats must be kept the same size. Having made your first pleat leave a smaller space and then continue like this all along the base of the first piece of material, pinning each pleat to the base ring; then pin the pleats into position along the top of the frame. Oversew to the frame as you did for the other lampshades (diag. 3). Complete all the pieces of material in turn, making the number of pleats the same in each panel of the frame. Join the material by folding in the new material to the last pleat in the used piece. As this shade has no lining you now turn back the raw edges and stitch over the double thickness of satin and then cut very closely (diag. 4).

This is the way to trim your lampshade using your $1\frac{1}{2}″$ strips, but of course this is optional. No doubt by now you will have your own ideas about trimmings. Double your material lengthways, right sides outside, and oversew to the base of the shade, so that when this is turned up it will form a cover for your stitching. The joins can be covered with small tabs of material. This method of trimming is illustrated in diags. 2 and 4 on page 11. This gives a nice neat finish.

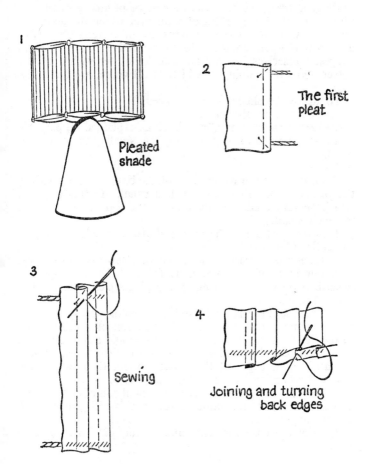

1

Pleated shade

2 The first pleat

3 Sewing

4 Joining and turning back edges

A PLEATED LAMPSHADE

ONE of the prettiest lampshades is this pleated style, shown in diag. 1, where we have the fullness of pleated georgette or ninon, and the lovely effect of satin over which the georgette has been worked. The trimmings are of velvet ribbon with a narrow old-gold edging. Many attractive colour schemes suggest themselves for this lampshade: oyster with a darker velvet, red with a lining of white, or all white, are but a few ideas.

To make the shade, you will need:

(*a*) A frame as shown in diag. 2.

(*b*) Georgette or ninon, calculated as explained on page 18.

(*c*) Velvet ribbon and an edging. A small piece of cotton wool.

Method:

1. Pleat along the lower edge of the bound frame, spacing the pleats a little more widely than usual. In this way you will have very much less material at the top, where the ring is much smaller.

2. Sew the pleats to the base and also to the lower ring of the collar (diag. 3).

3. Extend the pleats to the top collar, sew and cut closely.

4. Put in a pleated lining, as for the Coolie lampshade described on page 46, bringing the pleats well over the top ring, as in diag. 4.

5. The trimming is best assembled before being attached to the frame. You will need velvet ribbon of a width equal to the depth of the collar, and about one and a half times the circumference of the collar in length, to allow for gathering.

Gather both edges of the velvet ribbon, then attach the old-gold trimming to each edge, as diag. 5.

6. Sew this to the collar, placing a small roll of cotton wool along the inside of the gathered velvet; this will give it a well padded appearance.

7. Trim the base with the same velvet, put on as a plain binding.

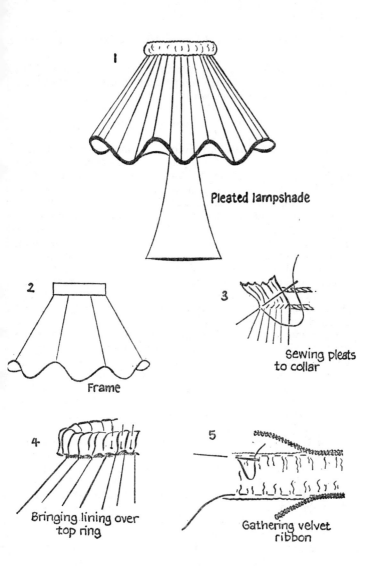

1

Pleated lampshade

2

Frame

3

Sewing pleats to collar

4

Bringing lining over top ring

5

Gathering velvet ribbon

A LAMPSHADE WITH A BALLOON LINING

As you have had some practice in different ways of making a cover, you will now feel competent to attempt a balloon lined shade. This is one which has a lining placed inside the frame, so that the bound wires cannot be seen. The method used is to prepare the cover and lining, but fix the cover to the frame first.

You will need a straight Empire or bowed Empire frame, a lining folded right sides together and a cover also folded in the same way. Place the folded cover against the frame and pin as already explained, pencil the line and remove it from the frame, and stitch the seams on the line, leaving raw edges. The lining is prepared in the same way, but when you take it off the frame, sew one seam at each side about $\frac{1}{8}''$ inside the pencil line (diag. 1). This will allow your lining to be slightly smaller than the outside of the frame and it should then be the correct size for fitting on the inside.

Having prepared the cover and lining, you are then ready to fix them on. Fix the cover as you have done in the previous shades, but the turnings at the top and base rings are cut quite closely, about $\frac{1}{4}''$, as you will not need any allowance for turning back the edges this time. Having attached the cover to the frame you are now ready to put in the lining. Cut the side turnings of this to $\frac{1}{4}''$ and then, holding the shade upside down, slip the lining inside and place the seams so that they each rest against a stave, and then pin at the top and at the base. All the pins must be placed on the inside of the frame (diag. 2). Place a few more pins round the top and base; you will have to cut the lining to allow it to fit round the frame fitting at the top (diag. 3). Now transfer all the pins to the outside, holding the material firmly and adjusting it where necessary. You will have to snip it at the top to allow it to come over the ring (diag. 4). When you are certain that there are no puckers or fullness left, oversew the lining to the outside, using the same method as before, turning back the raw edges and then cutting the material very closely. Trim in the usual way.

A balloon lining differs from a cover by the fact that it should stand away from the staves, and the finished effect should be quite smooth with no staves showing through the material.

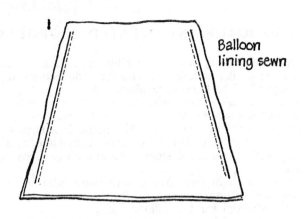

Balloon lining sewn

Lining placed inside frame

Base of shade

Lining cut at frame fitting

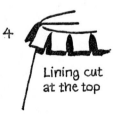

Lining cut at the top

BROCADE AND PLEATED GEORGETTE

ANOTHER exciting idea is to combine two panels of brocade, or other similar material, with the four side sections of pleated georgette. The lampshade illustrated in diag. 1 has panels of a royal blue satin, with pleated cream georgette. It is lined with a pale peach satin, and the trimmings are in cream, to tone with the georgette. The frame is a narrow shape, which is most suitable for a modern mantelpiece, as it will fit very well into a small space. To make the shade you will need:

(*a*) A straight oval frame, with two centre sections and four side sections.

(*b*) Material for the balloon lining.

(*c*) Material for the two panels, and for the pleated sections.

Method:

1. Having bound the frame, prepare the balloon lining in the usual way.

2. Sew on the panels as in diag. 2, and turn back the side seams, as diag. 3.

3. Cut off the length of georgette needed for the pleating, and then work in the same way as the Drum, except that, as the top ring is smaller than the base, the pleats on the top must overlap, to compensate for the difference in size.

4. Place the first pleat well over the raw edges of the panel, as in diag. 4.

5. Continue pleating until you come to the last stave, then turn under a small box pleat (diag. 5). This makes a neat finish.

6. Cut away all the edges to about $\frac{1}{4}$ inch, then the shade is ready for the lining.

7. Place your selected trimming round the top and the base.

The peach-coloured lining of this lampshade gives a pleasant warm light, which is needed to offset the coldness of the royal blue satin.

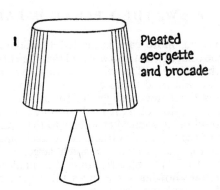

1 Pleated georgette and brocade

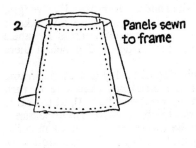

2 Panels sewn to frame

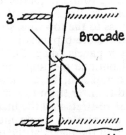

3 Brocade

Turning back side of panel

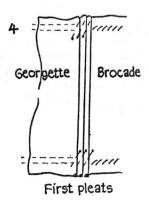

4 Georgette | Brocade

First pleats

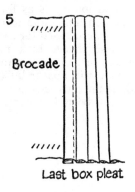

5 Brocade

Last box pleat

31

A SWATHED PLEATED LAMPSHADE

A LITTLE more care is needed to make a swathed pleated shade (diag. 1), but you will find that the effort is well rewarded, as the finished effect will look most expensive.

You will need a bowed Empire shaped frame, a lining and any of the materials suggested for pleating. Pin and sew your lining but do not fix it to the frame. Fix the cover first, the method being somewhat similar to the straight pleated Drum, but as the top of this frame is so much smaller than the base, your top pleats must be much larger and must overlap in order to fit the material into the smaller space. Cut your material allowing three times the circumference of the base and, as explained on page 18, allowance must be made for pulling round a quarter of the shade. Remove all selvedges, then pin the first pleat in position at the base and take it across to the top ring, stretching the material across $1\frac{1}{2}$ panels if there are 6 panels in the frame, or across 2 panels if there are 8 panels (diag. 2).

Continue pleating and pinning until 1 panel of the frame is completed, then remove the base pins each one in turn and transfer them to a slanting position (diag. 3), at the same time re-stretching the material to give a good firm appearance to the pleats. There must be the same amount of material used in the pleats at the top and base of each section (diag. 4). Sew the panel, and make sure that your stitches are catching in the binding at the top ring, as there is a considerable thickness to sew through. Each panel should be completed in turn, and joining is as for the straight pleated shade. Fix the balloon lining and trim the top and base rings.

The material used for swathed pleating should stretch well, and these shades look most satisfactory if covered in a georgette or a similar textured material, otherwise the top of the shade will appear bulky and thick. This type of lampshade is the most advanced you will have attempted, but the result will be well worth the trouble taken.

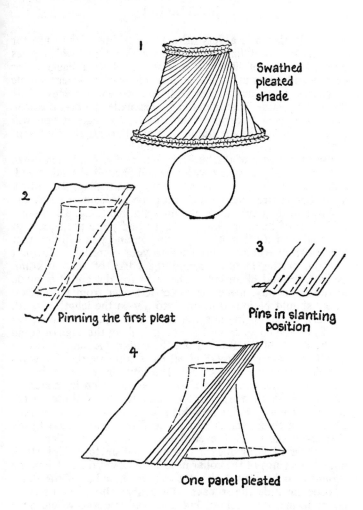

1

Swathed
pleated
shade

2

Pinning the first pleat

3

Pins in slanting
position

4

One panel pleated

33

A FLARED COVER IN BUCKRAM AND MATERIAL

WHITE buckram is a very attractive stiff material to use for lampshades, as it has a pleasant rough texture which gives good diffusion of light. It is also useful as a backing for cotton and other materials, and in this way it is very simple to change your lampshades with your colour schemes. The flared lampshade illustrated (diag. 1) is made in a bright cotton material over a buckram foundation. To make it you will need a 10″ Coolie type frame with a collar, an 18″ square of material and the same amount of buckram.

Find the centre of the buckram square and firmly pin down a 9″ length of fine string with a pencil fixed at the other end, and mark a circle lightly with your pencil (diag. 2). Mark a smaller centre circle which must be the same size as the collar, and then cut out on the lines marked (diag. 3). Damp this piece of buckram with a sponge and place the square of material over it (diag. 4). Iron this on and you will find that the buckram will be firmly fixed to your material. Now cut out the cotton material round the edges of the buckram, making a good clean cut. The strip for the collar is made in the same way, using the pieces left over from the circles. These should be joined in order to obtain the length needed.

Mark the base ring and the cover in 8 equal divisions; the marks on the cover should be about 1″ from the edge or equal to the depth of the frame from the collar. A simple way to divide the base ring into 8 equal parts is to use the side wires as guides for your marks. Slip the cover over the frame and attach it to the collar and also to the base ring by matching one of the pencil marks on the frame to one of those on the cover. Sew with a few invisible stitches (diag. 5). Now take all the matching marks round the frame and attach those. The result should be 8 even flares. Sew on the collar.

The trimming for this shade is more satisfactory if it is stuck on. Both rings of the collar need to be covered and trimming should also be placed about 1″ above the edge of the flares in order to hide the stitches. Of course, should you have a larger frame, the circle of buckram and material would have to be larger in proportion.

Experiment with new stiffeners as they come on the market.

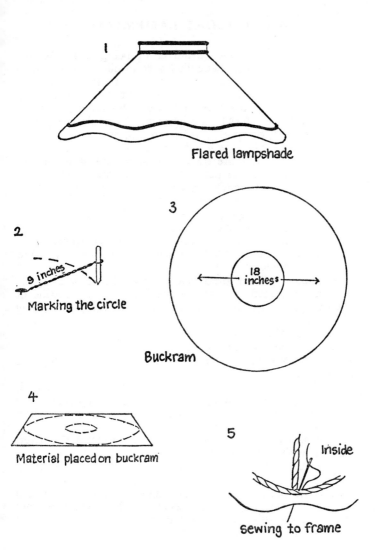

1

Flared lampshade

2

9 inches

Marking the circle

3

18 inches

Buckram

4

Material placed on buckram

5

Inside

sewing to frame

A PETTICOAT LAMPSHADE

This lampshade has the advantage of being removable for easy laundering. The shade illustrated in diag. 1 was worked in fine pink linen and decorated with pulled thread embroidery, which looks most effective when the light is on. The lining was in white, and the edge of this was bound with pink to match the cover. Any lightweight material would be suitable, including plain or spotted voile, muslin, etc.

To make the shade you will need:

(a) A straight Empire frame, which must first be bound.

(b) Material for the petticoat cover, equal to one and a half times the circumference of the lower ring, and the depth of the frame plus a few inches, to allow for a heading at the top and a hem at the base.

(c) Material for a lining.

(d) Bias binding for the base of the covered frame.

(e) Ribbon for threading through the heading, and a few press studs.

To make the lining, prepare a cover for the frame using the French seam method. Attach the lining to the outside of the frame, and finish the lower edge with the bias binding (diag. 2).

To make the petticoat cover:

1. Hem the sides and lower edge.

2. Turn over the top about $1\frac{1}{2}$ inches. (You will need more for a large frame.)

3. Make a casing for a ribbon along the top, as diag. 3.

4. Sew press studs along the outside of the top ring of the frame, placing two close together at one of the staves, as in diag. 4.

5. Attach their counterparts along the inside of the cover, starting with one at each end.

6. Run a ribbon through the casing, gathering it up to fit the top ring.

7. Fasten all press studs, matching those which are at each end of the cover with the two which are placed close together on the frame (diag. 5). Tie a bow.

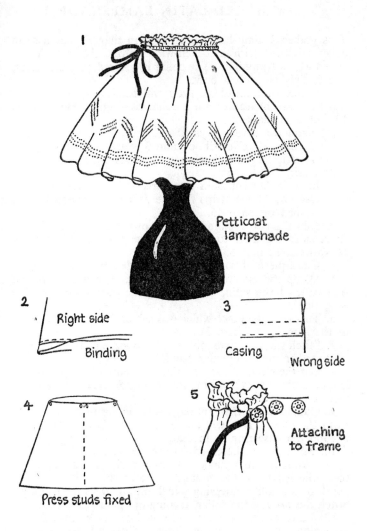

1

Petticoat lampshade

2 Right side

Binding

3 Casing

Wrong side

4 Press studs fixed

5 Attaching to frame

GATHERED SATIN LAMPSHADE

THIS gathered lampshade, illustrated in diag. 1, has a satin cover trimmed with a 2-inch-wide velvet ribbon which is edged with a trimming. The collar is covered with the velvet, and is finished with a bow.

To make the lampshade, you will need:

(a) A straight frame with a collar as diag. 2. This one is 10 inches in diameter.

(b) Satin for cover—$\frac{3}{4}$ yard.

(c) 2 yards of velvet ribbon and $3\frac{1}{2}$ yards of trimming.

(d) A strip of white buckram, 2 inches wide.

Method:

1. Bind frame; cut satin into three strips lengthways.

2. Use one of the strips for the lining; make and fit this as described on page 46.

3. Join the two remaining pieces of satin, placing the two short sides together, so that you have a length of material $1\frac{1}{2}$ yards × 12 inches.

4. Cut a piece of buckram, the same length, 2 inches wide.

5. Damp the buckram on one side, and iron it on to the right side of the satin, $\frac{1}{2}$ inch from the edge of one of the long sides.

6. Turn over the $\frac{1}{2}$ inch which was left, and fix to the buckram in the same way (diag. 3).

7. Stitch the velvet ribbon over the buckram, and then join all together into a circular band.

8. Cut the circular band so that it is equal in depth to the length of the staves from the lower ring of the collar, plus $2\frac{1}{4}$ inches.

9. Gather along the raw edge side of the material $\frac{1}{4}$ inch from the edge. This will allow the velvet border to extend beyond the base ring as in diag. 4.

10. Stitch this gathered edge to the lower ring of the collar.

11. From the material cut from the circular band, cut a piece the length of the circumference of the collar, and the depth of the collar, allowing $\frac{1}{2}$ inch on all edges for turnings. Stitch this around the collar, turning in the raw edges.

12. Catch down the cover on to the lower ring of the frame, arranging eight evenly spaced flutes. These stitches should be placed on the top edge of the velvet ribbon.

13. Trim both edges of the velvet ribbon and cover the collar with velvet, padding this with cotton wool. Trim the lower edge to match the border. Tie a bow and fix in position.

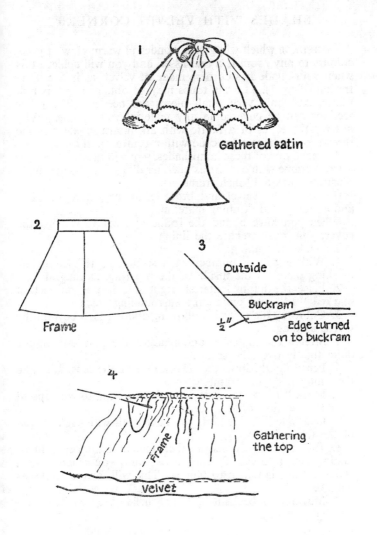

1

Gathered satin

2

Frame

3

Outside

Buckram

½" Edge turned
on to buckram

4

Frame

Gathering
the top

velvet

SHADES WITH VELVET CORNERS

A LAMPSHADE which will give a wonderful warm glow of jewel colours to any room is a real asset, and you will achieve this when your shade has corners made of velvet, as in the illustration (diag. 1). Lovely tones may be obtained in this rich fabric, and only very small pieces are needed. The other sections can be covered in any material you choose. Why not try the effect of a fabric with an untarnishable metallic thread, or perhaps a brocade with a centre motif?

To make one of these lampshades, you will need:

(a) A frame with corners as in either diags. 2 or 3; the shade illustrated has a 12-inch frame,

(b) Materials; velvet and brocade, about $\frac{1}{4}$ yard of each and about $\frac{1}{2}$ yard of lining material.

When you have bound the frame and before starting the cover, you must prepare the lining.

To make the lining:

1. With a pencil, number each section of the frame, by marking them on the inside of the top ring, as diag. 4.

2. Place the lining material, right side inside, on section marked " 1 ", and pin to the surrounding wires.

3. Cut away the material, allowing about 1 inch beyond the wires, as diag. 5.

4. Stretch the material, and readjust the pins until it fits quite tightly over the section.

5. Pencil lightly down the staves, remove the pins, and take the lining from the frame.

6. Mark " 1 " on the margin of the material, to correspond with that section of the frame.

7. Continue like this until you have dealt with each section of the frame in turn.

8. Tack all the sections together, matching the pencil lines, joining No. 1 to No. 2, and so on, until you reach No. 8, which in turn is joined to No. 1. This will form a circle, as diag. 6.

9. Machine or backstitch, $\frac{1}{8}$ inch inside the pencil lines.

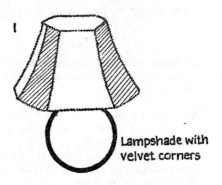

1 Lampshade with velvet corners

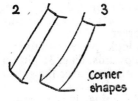 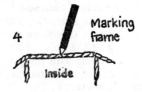

2 **3** Corner shapes

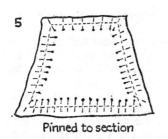

4 Marking frame
Inside

5 Pinned to section

6 Lining assembled

41

SHADES WITH VELVET CORNERS

The Cover

THE two larger panels of the frame are covered first, then the two smaller panels, and lastly the corners which are to have the velvet as covers.

Method:

1. Place the material over the panel, with the right side outside. Fix your first two pins on the straight of the material at the centre base and at the centre top of the panel (diag. 1). This is most essential if the fabric has a centre motif.

2. Continue to pin until the material is tightly stretched across the wires. Cut about one inch away from the outside of the section, then sew into the binding (diag. 2). Cut away close to the stitches. All the panels are worked in the same way, except of course the velvet corners.

To give the velvet corners a rich look, place the fabric on to the panels with the pile running upwards, diag. 3; pin and work as the other panels, this time stitching over the stitches already there.

THE LINING. Before putting in the lining, it is as well to cover any raw edges of the material on the staves with some kind of trimming; it is so much easier to do this while you can handle the lampshade freely. The base and the top will be trimmed later.

1. Insert the lining by matching the numbers on the material with those on the frame, as diag. 4.

2. Fix the first two pins at the base and at the top of the seams, making sure that they are placed against staves. Continue as for a balloon lining, and finish the top ring where the fitting joins it, as described on page 4.

3. Attach your trimming to the top and to the base rings. A tassel fringe looks well with this style of lampshade, but choose the fringe to match the velvet in colour, and a braid to tone with the other panels for a good effect.

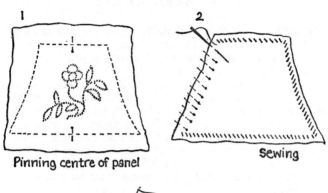

1

Pinning centre of panel

2

Sewing

3

Velvet

$\overline{\text{Pile}}$

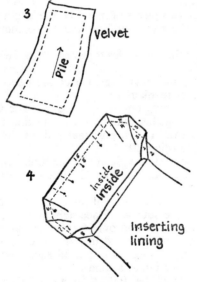

4

Inside

Inserting lining

A SECTIONAL LAMPSHADE
IN GLAZED CHINTZ

SOMETIMES it may happen that, owing to the nature of your material, or perhaps to the shape of the frame, you cannot use the usual methods of covering your lampshade. Glazed chintz is an example of this kind of material, and as it is sometimes very pleasing to match a lampshade to your furnishings, it is useful to know how to deal with this problem. All panels of the frame must be of the same shape and size to use this method. The fabric is placed on one part of the frame at a time, and attached to each part in turn. Usually one to three panels are covered with each piece of material. This depends on the shape of the frame; for the sake of clarity we shall take one panel. The frame must be bound.

Method:

1. Take two pieces of material, the length and width needed to cover the panel, adding about one inch on all sides for turnings.

2. With the right sides together, place the two pieces against one of the panels. Pin all round the wires, quite loosely to start with, and then stretch over the panel until you have a good fit, as in diag. 1.

3. Stitch down one of the staves; these stitches should be very close together and through both thicknesses of material.

4. Cut away the surplus material, as close to the stitching as possible (diag. 2).

5. Remove all the pins from the three other sides, open out the top material, then pin all round the outside wires, as in diag. 3.

6. Take another piece of material, the same size as one of those used previously. Place right sides together, pin over the section just sewn, and onto the frame, taking these pins right through the material and into the binding. Remove the pins from the lower piece, and pin all round the remaining wires. Deal with one pin at a time.

7. Sew down the stave, then cut as before.

8. When the first pinned section is reached, readjust the pins, if necessary, and sew down the stave. Cut closely, then pin the last section to this stitched stave.

9. Cut the material away to $\frac{1}{4}$ inch from the pins, turn under this amount, then sew with invisible stitches, as diag. 4. Finish the top and base as usual.

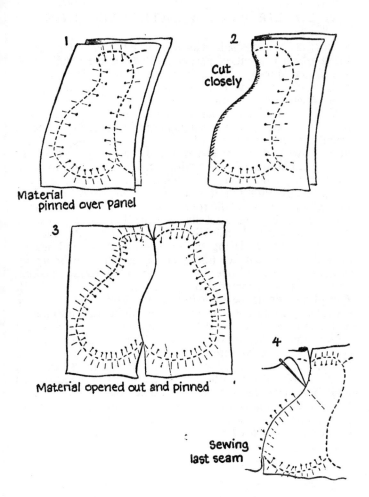

1

Material
pinned over panel

2

Cut
closely

3

Material opened out and pinned

4

Sewing
last seam

45

A COOLIE WITH A GATHERED LINING

SOMETIMES a lampshade may have a gathered lining, and a shape which lends itself particularly well is the Coolie type. The frame shown in the illustration is a Coolie without a collar. If the shade is a pendant the gathered lining will show when you look up into it.

You will need the usual amount of material for a cover. In order to assess the material you need for the lining, measure round the large ring and add turnings and the depth of the frame, also with a few inches added. Make your cover as for the balloon lined shade with simple seams, and fix it to the frame. When you have trimmed all the edges, take the lining material and join it into a continuous band, right sides inside, which will just fit round the lower ring. It is worth while measuring this carefully, as your lining will be useless if it is too tight and unsightly if it is too loose. Pin and sew this to the base, placing the seam on a stave, and sewing over the cover stitches (diag. 2). Then pull the lining up inside the frame and over the top ring to the outside, making small pleats in the material and pinning these in place (diag. 3). The pleats should be even in size and evenly placed. The easiest way to do this is to divide your lining first into halves and then into quarters, marking these quarters with pins, and do the same on the top ring. You will then be able to fit each section of material into its corresponding section on the frame. Sew in the usual way and trim closely (diags. 3 and 4).

The Coolie shape with a collar may also be lined in this way, but as all the Coolie type frames usually have larger lower rings compared with the other shapes, you must remember that if this ring measures more than 36″ round the circumference you will need two widths of 36″ wide material.

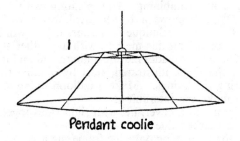

1

Pendant coolie

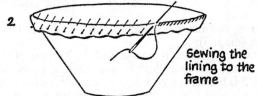

2

Sewing the lining to the frame

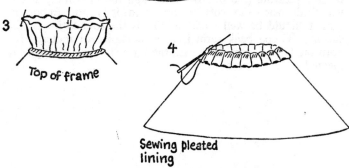

3

Top of frame

4

Sewing pleated lining

"SUNRAYS"

The Lining

THE sunray lampshade is an attractive style, which is well worth the little extra trouble of making. There are many variations, some combining plain pleating with panels of sunrays. Diag. 1 shows a bowed oval frame with sunray pleating. Once this technique is mastered, you will have no difficulty in combining this method with any other styles you choose. These lampshades require a lining and an interlining.

To make the shade illustrated, start by binding the frame and preparing the linings. Make a balloon lining and put it aside. To make the interlining:

1. Prepare as for a cover, i.e. with right sides together, and sewn on the marked line.

2. Place the interlining onto the frame, as a cover, pinning round the top and the base as usual.

3. Cut the material at the top and at the base of all the staves, as in diag. 2.

4. Bring the material under the wires and over to the front, and pin (diag. 3).

5. Sew firmly on to the outside of the binding of the frame.

6. Cut the material close to the stitches, as in diag. 4.

With this interlining now in position, the lampshade is ready for the pleating (see p. 50). Although the interlining shows very little when the work is completed, it is most important that it should be well made, as this is the foundation of the sunray. Crepe back satin is a good choice of material for both the linings, especially with the satin showing through the pleated cover.

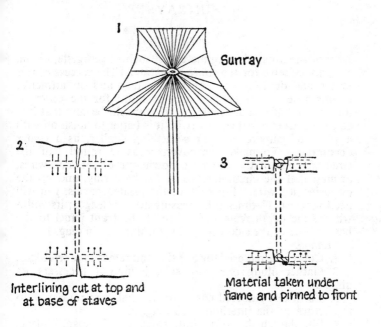

1

Sunray

2

Interlining cut at top and
at base of staves

3

Material taken under
frame and pinned to front

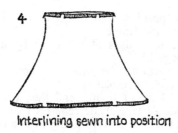

4

Interlining sewn into position

The Cover

ANY of the usual pleating materials, such as georgette, ninon, etc., are suitable for the sunray pleating. The success of this lampshade depends on accurate pleating and an attractive colour scheme. A good choice of motif for the centre is important. If you are making this yourself, be sure that it is as perfect as is possible, otherwise it is better to finish off with a piece of guipure lace, or something similar, as a centre decoration. To make the cover, measure round half the circumference of the top ring, down one of the side wires, around half the circumference of the base ring, and up the opposite side wire. For each of the pleated panels, you will need material $1\frac{1}{2}$ times this measurement in length; its width will be the depth from the centre of the front panel to the base of one of the side wires, plus turnings, as in diag. 1.

Method:

1. Cut off the material for one side and remove the selvedges.

2. Gather along one long side, joining if necessary, as diag. 2.

3. Form this gathered edge into a small circle. Sew into the centre of the interlining, as diag. 3.

4. Pin the outside edge into small evenly spaced pleats (diag. 4).

5. Sew into position and cut closely. Repeat on the opposite side of the frame.

6. Cover the raw edges at the sides by using the finish described on page 12.

7. Attach a motif to the gathered centre; allow this to cover the raw edges completely.

8. Insert the balloon lining, and then trim the top and base. This style of lampshade requires that careful thought be given to the trimming. Overdoing this can spoil the whole effect, as the lampshade itself is decorative enough without much further trimming.

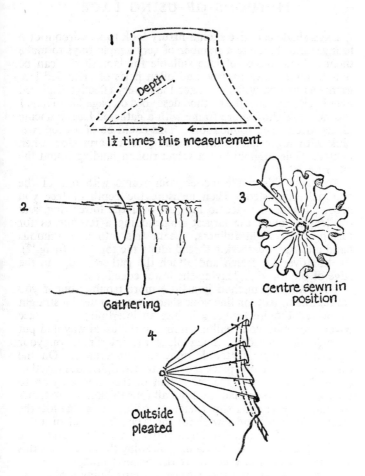

1

Depth

1½ times this measurement

2

Gathering

3

Centre sewn in
position

4

Outside
pleated

51

METHODS OF USING LACE

A LACE shade can give such a luxury look to a bedroom or a lounge, and there are a number of very simple ways to make them. Small pieces of lace suitable for lampshades can be bought quite inexpensively, and often parts of discarded lace garments can be utilized. Lace looks very effective if placed over buckram, using the method described on page 34. Diag. 1 shows a straight Empire frame with a gathered lace flouncing placed over a silk foundation. This could be of a deep rose pink with white lace, which would give a warm glow when lighted. The original had a velvet ribbon binding round the top ring.

To make this shade, cover your frame with one of the materials suggested. Then measure the depth of lace you need, allowing the lace to fall just over the lower ring, and the length round the largest ring, adding a few inches for turnings and slight fullness. Seam this into a continuous band and run a gathering thread along the top edge (diag. 2). Fit this over the frame and attach the gathered edge to the edge of the top ring, leaving the lower edge loose.

The following method is a little more trouble, but if you would like to balloon line your shade, you will need a straight or bowed Empire frame, a lining, an interlining and a lace cover. Prepare your balloon lining in the usual way and put it aside until needed. Then place the interlining on your work-table, single material, right side uppermost. On the top of this to one side place the lace, folded right sides together (diag. 3). Fold over the other half of the interlining on to the top of the folded lace and pin all four thicknesses together so that they cannot slip (diag. 4). Place this against the frame, pin, mark and sew as for the " Quickie " but turn this cover completely inside out and you will then have your lace on the outside with the interlining showing through. Put this over the frame and then insert the balloon lining.

An ecru or a deep cream lace over a satin lining looks most effective when the lamp is unlighted, but is even more so when the light is on, as the pattern of the lace shows up so well.

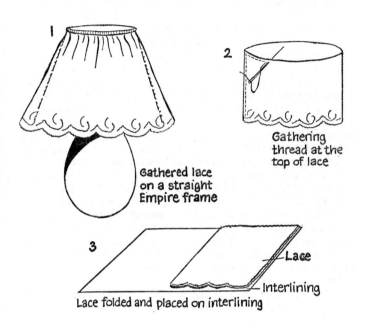

1

Gathered lace on a straight Empire frame

2

Gathering thread at the top of lace

3

Lace

Interlining

Lace folded and placed on interlining

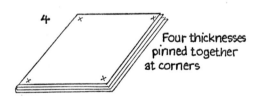

4

Four thicknesses pinned together at corners

BEDHEAD LAMPSHADES

BEDHEAD lampshades may be made of small pieces of material or cuttings which remain from other sewing jobs. These remnants can be used to make very attractive shades. Some of these frames are suitable for firm materials, such as buckram or one of the plastics which are mentioned on page 14; others, such as the frame illustrated in diag. 1, look well when covered in a fabric. You will find that these frames have a fitting at the back, which is in two parts, as in diag. 2. The narrow part at the top should be left uncovered. The lower part is best covered in a double piece of white material with a small section of asbestos slipped in between; this prevents the heat from the lamp damaging the bedhead. Pieces of asbestos, of a size suitable for this purpose, may be obtained for a few pence.

To cover the front, using small pieces of material:

1. Pin your material over the centre panel, as diag. 3. Oversew firmly in position, cut away closely at the side wires.

2. Cover the remaining panels in the same way, placing the second row of stitches over those already there.

3. Turn back the edges in the usual way, then place a trimming down the staves and along the top and base. It is as well to keep this trimming rather narrow, as the whole effect may be spoiled by a heavy appearance.

Small cuttings of georgette or ninon may be utilized by pleating one section of a frame, as shown in diag. 4. The remaining panels could be covered in another material.

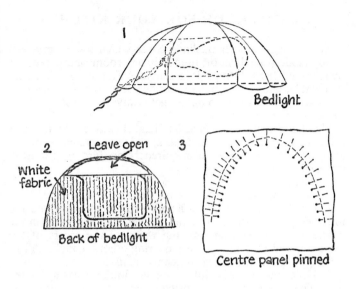

1

Bedlight

2

White
fabric

Leave open

Back of bedlight

3

Centre panel pinned

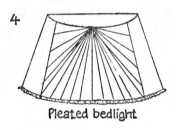

4

Pleated bedlight

A LAMPSHADE FOR YOUR KITCHEN

THIS is a removable lampshade cover which looks very well in any modern kitchen, or, in fact, in any room where frequent washing of light fittings is essential. The cover is easily removable, and if it is made in a fine cotton fabric it will give a good light while helping to get away from the working aspect of the kitchen.

The lampshade illustrated in diag. 1 was made to fit a frame of the type shown in diag. 2, which measured 10 inches across the base. Materials required: One-third yard cotton material, elastic and tape.

Method:

1. Paint the frame; there is no need to bind it first.

2. Cut the material into a length sufficient to fit round the lower ring in one dimension and the depth of the frame in the other, allowing it to fit into the waist, to the centre of the top ring, and also under the base ring, about 1 inch. Allow turnings on all these measurements (diag. 2).

3. Form the material into a circle. Make a casing at the top, wide enough to take a piece of tape, and another casing at the other side to take the elastic (diag. 3).

4. Thread some elastic through this last casing, which should be long enough to fit under the base ring.

5. Thread some tape through the top casing. Draw this up as tightly as possible. The opening should be just clear of the light fitting.

6. Attach ties at the seam, in the correct position for the narrow waist of the frame, as in diag. 4.

7. Slip the cover over the frame and tie a bow, pulling the cover into evenly spaced pleats.

As a variation of this lampshade you could have ties of a contrasting colour to the cover. But one-third yard of material allows for self material ties when covering a 10-inch frame.

*   *   *

The author and publishers are indebted to HOME MAGAZINE *for permission to reproduce this design and the instructions.*

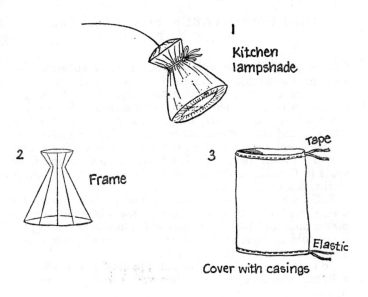

1 Kitchen lampshade

2 Frame

3 Tape

Elastic

Cover with casings

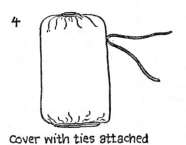

4 Cover with ties attached

SHADES SUITABLE FOR ADAPTED
WINE BOTTLES

CHAMPAGNE and other wine bottles can make attractive and sometimes uncommon additions to our more usual lampstands. Take your choice of the following larger-sized champagne bottles: Magnums, Jeroboams, Rehoboams, Methuselahs, Salamanazars, Balthazars, or perhaps a Nebuchadnezzar. All these, and many others, can be converted to great advantage by the use of adapters. These cost only a few shillings; some have a flex at the side, as in diag. 1, others require a hole to be made in the side of the base of the bottle, as in diag. 2. A glazier will usually do this for you.

Raffia with its pleasant natural colour lends itself well for shades used with bottles. There is also obtainable now a plastic raffia in beautiful colours which has the advantage of being sold in bundles composed of one length; this makes joining unnecessary in most cases.

To make the lampshade illustrated in diag. 3, you will need a frame with straight side wires and a bundle of natural raffia.

Method:

1. Pick some good pieces of raffia, discard any thin strands. Open out each length as you work.

2. Tie one end to one of the rings, then bind firmly over the outside of the frame, and over the other ring. Continue like this, covering the end which was left as you work (diag. 4). Always begin and end at a ring.

3. When the whole of the frame is covered, weave in the last and, using a darning needle to help you.

4. Decorate the top and base with plaited raffia (diag. 5). This may be bought ready made, and, as it is not expensive, it is hardly worth while making this yourself.

Although the above directions are intended for natural raffia, they can still apply to plastic raffia, but in this case it would not be necessary to decorate with the plait. When working with this material, other contemporary shapes of frames may be used, and interesting decorative effects can be obtained by using a combination of two colours.

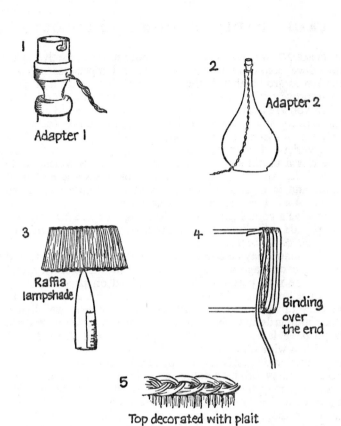

1 Adapter 1

2 Adapter 2

3 Raffia lampshade

4 Binding over the end

5 Top decorated with plait

LAMP SHADES—DESIGN AND COLOUR

A PLEASANT way to make your rooms more attractive is to introduce colour into them with your lampshades. When the lamps are lit, then is the time for their warmth and glow to improve your colour scheme. It is most important, too, when you are planning the lighting of your rooms, to consider the placing and position of the fittings, as well as the shape and the design of the lampshades. Bulbs may be obtained in a variety of colours, and these give a pleasing soft light. There is a useful small mushroom-shaped bulb which, while it takes less space than the usual-sized bulb, gives a very good light, and is a great advantage when your lampshade is so shaped that it comes close to the fittings.

To give a good light and a welcoming look in a hall make a lampshade as in diag. 1. Choose a warm colour for this, or use one of the coloured bulbs.

This shape may be covered with material, using the method described on page 44. An alternative idea is to work round the frame with plastic raffia, as described on page 58.

For a lounge or sitting-room you will need lampshades to be decorative as well as useful, so you may need wall lights, floor standards and table lamps. For needlework and reading, a portable lamp, with a shade giving a well-directed light and lined with white for good reflection, is best. The shade illustrated in diag. 2 is made of pleated board*, which is obtainable in many bright colours, and lined with white. Floor standards may be in modern designs, which throw the light upwards and also downwards for reading. The shade illustrated in diag. 3 could be pleated or plain material.

For the dining-room a pendant fitting over the dining table, directing the light on to the centre of the table, is shown in diag. 4. The larger shade could be of a contemporary cotton, and the smaller one in a plain white material, throwing the light down onto the table.

* "Pleated board" is the trade name for pleated or laminated linen prepared paper or imitation parchment.

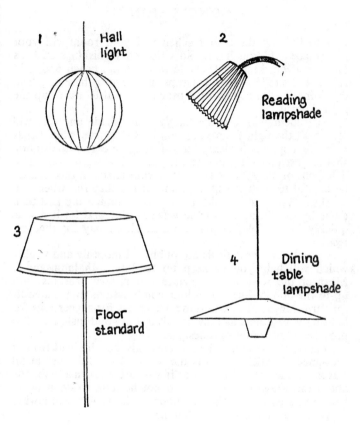

1 Hall light

2 Reading lampshade

3 Floor standard

4 Dining table lampshade

CONCLUSION

TRY to link up the colour scheme of your room with your lampshade. If you have cold coloured furnishings such as blue or green, keep your shade to the pink, peach and gold tones, and similarly if your lampshade cover is blue or green, try lining it with a pink or a peach material to warm up the light from it.

Experiment with one startlingly white shade and this will reflect all the light from your lamp. Of course, white needs to be kept spotlessly clean, but this is quite easy with a fabric shade—just place it sideways into a bowl of warm water and detergent or soap flakes and rotate your shade in this, but do be careful to hold the fitting and not the material when you do this. To rinse it, hold it under the running tap and then tie it by the fitting on to the washing line and let it dry as quickly as possible; choose a warm blowy day for the best results.

A number of periodicals are published monthly and weekly which will help you to keep up to date with lampshades. Most of the women's magazines run regular features with up-to-the-minute ideas in colour combinations and materials for furnishings. Look in these magazines for suggestions for lighting your home, as they are always in good taste and also provide details of current designs.

Finally, the best satisfaction can only be obtained from a well-finished article which is the result of careful work at all stages of the job. Therefore, if you are the least unhappy about any stage of the work do not hesitate to do it again before you go any further, as poor workmanship will always be reflected in the finished lampshade.

A NOTE ON STOCKISTS

Materials and lampshade frames may be obtained from many craft shops, but it may be helpful to you to have the names of the following stockists:

John Lewis & Co. Ltd, Oxford Street, London W.1 (and other stores in the John Lewis Partnership).
Homecraft Supplies Ltd, 27 Trinity Road, Balham, S.W.17.
Fred Aldous Ltd, P.O. Box 135, 37 Lever Street, Manchester 1, M60 1UX.
The Arts and Crafts Shop, 10 Byram Street, Huddersfield, Yorks.
Atlas Handicrafts Ltd., P.O. Box 385, Spring Alley, Manchester M60 4AV

* * *